Senses

Contents

Written by Catherine Veitch

Illustrated by Karl West

Eyes

You see with your eyes.

Look at this classroom.

What can you see in the classroom?

chair   book   clown

pens   blocks

Ears

You hear with your ears.

What can you hear on the farm?

duck   sheep   cow

chicken   cat

Nose

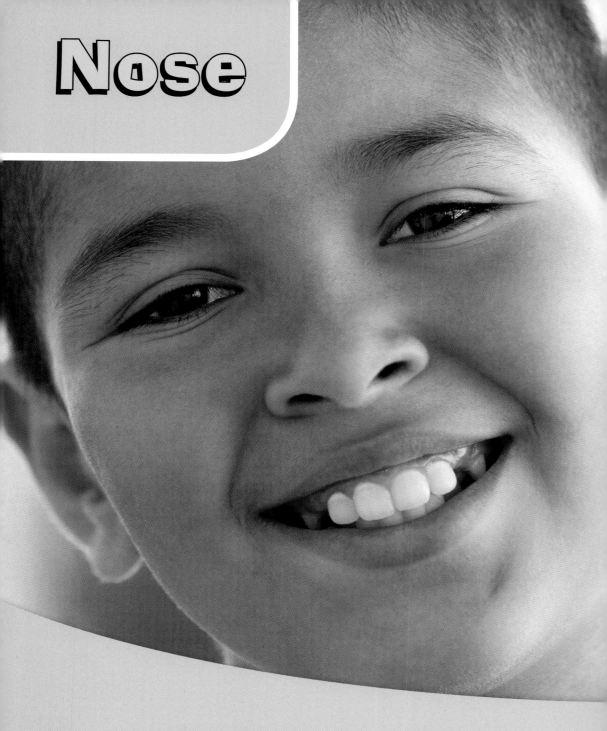

You smell with your nose.

Look at this bathroom.

What smells good
in the bathroom?

shampoo   soap   wet dog

mud   flower

Tongue

You taste with your tongue.

Look at this shop.

What tastes good in the shop?

milk sandwich lemons plums

Hands

You touch with your hands.

Look at this bedroom.

What feels soft in the bedroom?

train set   doll   bed

lamp   socks